Seraphim

Caron Chacko

RIGI PUBLICATION

Seraphim

BY

Caron Chacko

Originally published in India

ISBN: 978-93-89540-02-4 (Paperback)

978-93-89540-03-1 (eBook)

Published by RIGI PUBLICATION

777, Street no.9, Krishna Nagar
Khanna-141401 (Punjab), India
Website: www.rigipublication.com
Email: info@rigipublication.com
Phone: +91-9357710014, +91-9465468291

Index

Mother

O'er the universe He looked,
While under the stars He stood.
'All I need is a friend,' said He,
'Cause I've been alone all day long.'

He looked towards the stars galore,
They stretched a billion light years and more.
Pluck one from the skies He did,
Careful as ever, 'Oh, what a beautiful thing!'

'Think!' He said, 'What should I molden,
With this tiny star, so fragile and golden?'
He thought and thought and racked His brain,
Never did He feel so helpless and weak.

Then a smile crept onto His face,
It was in a flash, at an alarming pace.
Twinkle His eyes did,
Like the zillion stars across the sky

He bent His face to see the star,
With excitement that can never mar.
Slowly did He close His eyes,
And kiss the little thing so bright.

‘Oh!’ was all that escaped His lips,
For a pain had shot through His ribs.
A hand over His eyes He kept,
To keep Himself from being blown to bits.

Opened He His eyes then,
Shocked to see pretty women,
He gasped as they spiraled quickly,
Out of His sight, up, up, and away.

They landed on Earth, a lovely place,
And started a whole new human race,
Of females, so wise and kind,
That people so very liked.

Cooked, washed and worked did they,
But never tired, never they lay.
They labored in pain and suffering,
For the joy of the people around them.

He looked from above and saw a sight,
That never He would see, on another night.
‘Mother!’ cried a little girl,
To the little wonder that He had sent.

The First Man I Loved

He kissed me on my forehead,
Took my hand,
lead me,
taught me to take my first steps over troubled waters.

He teared up at my first laugh,
One day, showed me the picture of a giraffe,
and said, "Honey, the sky is your limit."

He clothed me in the choicest of dresses,
Every twirl of mine he cherishes,
"No, she hasn't grown up, she's still daddy's little girl."

He bought me my first book,
Watched me as, for the first time, through its pages I took a look.
Not knowing that one day,
I'd give him my very first book.

He gave me a shoulder to cry on,
Sang me to sleep; each day a different song.
Gazing at me lovingly as I slept,
Brushing the hair out of my eyes,
Whispering, "Good night."

Thank you, Appa.

Tiptoe

Stars twinkle from their adorned keep,
Through human minds mortal nightmares seep.
Ahoy, there stands a lonesome child,
With drooping eyes and little feet so very tired.
Trembling as he paces up the light-forsaken road,
Almost crouching, the cause, an invisible load.
'One more step, and you'll be fine,'
Perhaps, tonight, up the stairs of heaven he would climb.
T'was a time when human hearts seemed frozen,
Help was something that had been buried, but had not risen.
An ever-empty stomach and rapidly-weakening limbs,
Sat by a mongrel, as slowly his vision dims.
Nay, he had no mother, no father,
And certainly, no sympathy from the piercing eyes around him could he gather.
No one to call his,
No one to spend time with.
Heavens above gaily laughs at his plight,
Not one to care, have we all forgotten what is right?

Euthanasia

Call it 'mercy killing',
Call it whatever you want.
But it's our dreams you are stealing,
We have to live with it till we turn to sand.

Forget about the money,
All we need is a full heart.
Maybe we'll be homeless, but honey,
With passion we will never part.

Society says, "Look at Patricia,
She earns by the second."
Nah, Hitler didn't wield the real euthanasia,
The real thing happens in our homes, every minute, every moment.

Feminism

Feminism is a fortress
that women built
for a world called
'Utopia'.

Half Empty

Are you so full of ice
that you do not remember how to put the light back in my eyes?
Blue, blue, black and blue,
You've beaten the life out of me, every part I touch is a bruise.
Me, you never had chosen to choose.

Judas

He,
was supposed to shield me.
In turn, my body he scarred.
My soul's cocoon he marred.

He touched me everywhere,
I never knew I'd lost my way and entered a predator's lair,
Never again will I be the same,
He abandoned me on the shores of pain.

Defiled,
I'll never get back my sane mind.
My reserve of tears has run out,
From myself, even the shattered pieces of my heart has fallen out.

"You touched me everywhere."
Without him, how well I would've fared.
I don't know what to do,
Give me, give me just one clue.

Love

He was everything I wanted.
But no, I did not fall
in love with him.
I fell in love,
with loving him.

Medicine to the Soul

Fix my soul, for it is broken,
The threads that bind it, I have to tear it open.
On my feelings you have trodden,
The queen's kingdom, thus, has fallen.

You do not know what I have lost,
Imbecile! Your malignant façade I will no longer host.
A spear protrudes from within, no, a double-edged sword,
Take away the pain, this thing that you have caused.

I laugh my way through life,
I see it, I see the knife.
Purge me with divinity; wash away all my strife,
I probably should pay a heart-stopping price.

Mistake. Sorry. Repeat.

Mistake after mistake I do,
Breaking, dismantling every single rule,
God, when will I ever learn?
Every folly, every misstep burns
all those in my path
And then I have to face their wrath.
Aye, it is all fun and games,
Until I say, "Whoops, I did it again."

The Angel Who Fell

High above the heavens he flew,
With his wings a little askew.
For he was an angel so serene and pure,
He kneeled down before the Lord in all grandeur.

Slicing through the clouds he soared,
Doing errands as fast as a dart hitting a dartboard.
Pain in the most excruciating form went down his spine,
As his wings had been torn apart, the cause a sharp vine.

Down he fell, down to the earth,
A place full of joy and mirth.
He touched down in a forest so green and spry,
Filled with creatures of various kinds.

Looked around he did,
Under the trees, a universe lived.
Far away he could see obscure shadows,
Of things so tall and not-so-narrow.

'Do you know the way to heaven?' the angel implored,
To the beast before him, with horns that gored.
'Moo, moo,' said the beast,
'I do not know the way to heaven, all I know is to whip up a feast.'

'And you, oh creature of hairy nature,
Do you know the way to the abode of the Maker?'
'Mew, mew,' spoke the critter,
'I do not know the way to heaven, all I know is to make confetti and glitter.'

'You creature of extreme ugliness,
Do you have a way in mind?' probed the angel with sarcastic loveliness.
'Hee-Haw! Yes I do!' said the creature,
'If you wish it with your heart, you must be truly eager.'

Nothing surprised the angel as much as this,
And he went and gave the creature a kiss.
He thanked and thanked him profusely,
Learned he not to judge by beauty.

Flashed a light so bright and blinding,
Up the stairs of heaven he went, climbing.
The angel vanished from plain sight,
Up, up, and away in the starry twilight.

The condition on Earth was very forlorn,
For the angel they loved so much was gone,
When, lo! He came before them,
The throng of brutes began to thrum.

Gifts he did bring out,
The creatures streamed around him, all devout,
'I have to go my friends,
See you in the coming week-ends.'

Flitted to the doors of heaven he did,
He understood a thing so true and candid.
'Treat everyone fairly,' murmured he,
'Do not judge by beauty, inside you must see.'

Prosopis Cineraria

Head held high,
Boughs spread wide
Majestic are its looks, observing everything that passes by,
From a 'ghutra'-clad Arab to a camel's sigh.
But how does it look so green,
Subject to the boiling hot sun and the air so very mean,
Children plucking away every leaf and;
Men cutting them off from their land.
"Forgive them for what they do,"
A resounding plea to all those who rule.
'Year of Tolerance' it is,
But there is something – something, we miss.
Cutting off the ghaf won't help,
They are a symbol of tolerance, of love, it is them we should help.

Psycho

Hi.
Can I
tell you why
I killed my wife?

She was
beautiful, managed the wars
in us. Her pretty eyes on gleaming cars.
Her build as tall as centaurs.

My mind did not
like it. Her life I sought.
I'm sorry, it was for naught.
I loved her, for her my heart fought.

Confusing, isn't it?
My mind and my body do not fit.
I've defies all writs,
God, help me find my first-aid kit.

Rain, Rain, Go Away

Pitter, patter,
Windows bejeweled with the Queen's finest,
A wonder inside held a bundle of life that mattered,
A temptation for wandering cicadas to conclude who was loudest.

Pitter, patter,
Tearful eyes and smiles undiminished,
The wee baby gurgled and laughed and its eyes it battered,
Tidings of joy heralded the minute.

Plop, plop, plop,
Shades of black under the eyes begin,
A wheel set in motion, an unstoppable clock,
'Rock-a-by, baby,' thus they sing.

Plop, plop, plop,
Darting through the gaudy plants moisture-clad,
A laughter rising, as if life never had stopped,
Time granted them love, and no reason to be sad.

Grey clouds wafting gracefully,
'Mommy, I'm hurt!' set once again the pain they so forcefully kept away,
Ice-creams and kisses offered aplenty,
They held him tight, and there he stayed.

Drops on the glass pane,
Murmuring algorithms incomprehensive,
Sits a child already bestowed with wrinkles and an ever-growing mane,
Grudgingly ripping packets of almonds, a ritual done to make oneself more pensive.

Drops on the glass pane,
Knees hurting from prayers to Him up above,
Her heart, a recent devotee for the sake of her blood's claim,
Tears bequeathed to one she was proud of.

Sweet, blessed, beads of bliss,
Cheers to all for a life so wondrous!
The little boy, now a man, his hard work he reminisce,
For now he earned his own bread, had his own purpose.

Sweet, blessed, beads of bliss,
Never had their eyes been filled with tears, not of pain, but of delight,
Lifted from despair's abyss,
Smile they did, all they needed was a worthy bride.

Thunder and lightning,
Frailty beheld their now-old limbs,
Whispers and connivance frightening,
A secret threatened to be told, all hope it dims.

Shattered windows and uprooted trees,
The Rain God furiously bursting out of the skies,
A wretched spectacle the people around sees,
All they do is shake their heads and sigh.

Angry drops of rain,
'Father, Mother, we're done looking after you,'
Deserted two bodies, their hearts filled with pain,
Once their little boy, now he had grown and become
someone new.

Wistful sounds of night led them away,
Eyes gleaming with tears, a road of darkness before them
lay,
Turning back, pleading him to let them stay,
But cold, hard, eyes, revulsion they betray.

The Words of a Friend

I laughed at her
when she said
that she understood
the poems
we read
about pain and heartbreak.
"What do you know,"
I said.
"You're happy, right?"
"Believe me, you have
no idea."
She said,
"I have had no love life.
But I sure
have had
a heartbreak."
That
shut me up.

Scars of Your Love

The mirror said it all,
A wounded animal, I had taken fall after fall.
Belief was all that I had,
Oh, now that's gone too, leaving me half-mad.
Body aching,
Tired of a life filled with scuffling,
I lifted my head
to look at the mess before me, who made those eyes look so dead?
Once filled with laughter,
At you they gazed and fluttered.
Bones on my flesh like pokers from within,
My torso streaked with mud, I stood there, musing.
I decorated the scars you gave with pieces of my heart,
Thought it was okay, thought you were God's work of art.
Lies!
All that's left of me now,
Are the scars of your love.

Taboo

Shh! Don't say that!
What will people think?
Don't tell you like black,
Quick! Change it to pink!

Don't say what?
I will do what I fancy, say what I perceive.
It is not shame I lack,
A broad mind is what you need.

Pull those shorts down,
What is this? A piercing?
Darling, you are expected to wear dresses and flowing gowns,
It is society you're playing with.

Don't wear what?
No expectations, I'm no princess in sparkles,
Call me a soldier at heart,
I know no society, I count my own marbles.

Put that book aside,
What are you even doing?!
Come help me cook, stand beside,
Hey, hey, STOP daydreaming!

I'm sorry, I don't quite understand,
Must I live as a human gone passive?
I will not stand beneath any man,
Read I will, of my own accord I'll live.

To all those out there, who stand against women empowerment.

Someone Like You

Missing you was never part of the plan.
Forgetting an ugly scar, I never can.
Told me to stay silent,
While around me, you built a narcissistic tent.
"I feel scared, honey."
"Stop worrying for once, the world is always sunny."
But I'm okay,
I guess I never wanted you to stay,
Counting stars and the planets beyond,
Has helped kill the you in me, thank God.
Sorry this didn't work out, sorry this didn't blaze,
Still I walk on this road, trying to find someone like you in life's haze.

What is Beauty?

Asking, waiting,
Never replying.
"Mirror, mirror, on the wall,
Who's the fairest, of them all?"
Restricted and rigid,
The notion of modern-day beauty has made all our hearts downright frigid.
White, black, yellow or brown,
All their heads are adorned with invisible, unique crowns.
When will humanity ever learn?
For a diverse and unconventional world we yearn.
But we are incorrigible,
Our stigmas and prejudices, all are so very formidable.
Thin waists and fair faces,
What about the rest, don't they deserve praises?
Plump lips and sharp jaws,
Why can't you just look beyond our invisible flaws?
A good figure and a good heart,
Darling, are millions of miles apart.
In a world full of evening gowns and six-inch heels,
Can we not be carried away by fake smiles, please?
There's no definition of perfect,
All those fairness creams and syringes of Botox, I beg you to chuck them.
Within all of us is a cover girl,
An oyster for a home, every single woman is a priceless pearl.

Wings

Barren and empty was my soul,
Thank you, for making me feel whole.
From monochrome to colour,
My life has changed, you make my heart flutter.

Where Are You Now?

I fixed your broken heart,
In return, you broke mine into parts.
Where are you now when I need you?
Prove that I wasn't a fool.

I stitched your heart back together with the threads of our dreams,
And now, mine's cut open, you split its seams.
Where are you now that I want you?
Save me before I dissolve into pools of blue.

I made your heart near to perfect,
And that has caused mine heart to plummet.
Where are you now when I want to see you?
Please tell you love me too.

What Do I Do?

Should I go with my heart's desire
and face consequences dire?
Or should I do what my parents think is best,
And work without any zest?

War

The blood raged in my veins,
like a bloody, violent war.
The world ignored my pain,
While I counted my ugly scars.

One spark starts a fire,
Blinking back tears, I unsheathed my sword.
No, this mortal body will not tire,
Of snapping down each of my darkest nightmares' chords.

There's one thing blindingly clear,
That I am,
A god-damn warrior.

Unlove

I wish
there was
someway to
reverse the love
I had for one.
I wish
I could pull back
the strings of devotion
I had so lovingly
wound around him,
dreaming,
that one day,
he'd do the same to me.
He
never
did.

Tripping

I stumbled upon love
by accident
on one of those days
when I sat,
thinking about
blushing cheeks
and a 6-month old belly.

Some Other Me

It was on that one day
that some other me
erupted from my soul,
like an astral self
that was waiting,
waiting to be released
since birth.
Looking,
a smirk on her face.
Laughing at my pain
which was once hers.
Now she's gotten rid of the bane.

Smile, Please!

Just so you know,
You might be gone any day, even tomorrow.
Girl, flash those thirty-two beauties,
To amaze people you will never, ever cease.
Yeah, this world's not all about rainbows or sunshine,
I, for one, can't always be on cloud nine.
But when you look up and see storm clouds,
Just wait for the rain, its pattering sound.
Hey, stretch those facial muscles,
With your heart, darling, you don't have to tussle.

I'm Fine

There's a beauty to life,
(Makes me want to take the knife)
Caring friends take away all its strife.
(Toxic relations are the cause of my cries)
Mom and dad love me to no end,
(It's been years since my heart has had a mend)
They tell me, "Follow your passion, you to the doors of education we will send."
(From these lies, my dreams I defend)
Yes, life's a rollercoaster ride,
(It's me turning back, looking at all those comments so very snide)
The laws of man I've never defied.
(Hello world, I'm not even close to 'just fine')

Help

Cold nights come and go,
But this one goes rather slow.
Twilight shadows creep in,
As her soul crashes from within.

Mauled,
She watches herself being sold.
Stripped of dignity and all hopes of being alive,
'Give me what I want, name a price.'

Stars that have gone dark,
A musician without his harp,
Planting feet after feet in front of her,
Wilted, a drooping flower.

Don’t Look Inside

People talk about
our perfect smiles,
Just a camouflage
for sins and lies.
Pretty curtains
and fairy lights,
Only God knows all
that we well hide.
Their blank stares are enough
to shush our cries,
Trapped inside concrete bars,
Has the world gone blind?
Hearts they’ve turned to stone,
twice we’ll die,
Handshakes all along
a façade we provide.
Smile for the camera
don’t show your dark side,
Hug your brother now,
Or you’ll pay a price,
Kill him later on
And we’ll never mind.
Sadly floating through
the paths amplified
with broken pieces of
our souls cast aside.

Wedding bells ring loud
For the Devil's bride,
White is what we wear, it's
black inside.
Can't escape from this,
No suicide,
Don't look through our veils,
You'll be horrified.

Diamonds

A black sky
in a milky white expanse.
Right in front of me,
Two diamonds shone,
watery,
crystal clear,
beautiful, oh, so beautiful.

Claustrophobic

"Be a doctor!"
"Be an engineer!"
If anything other than these you foster,
Haha, at you we will sneer.

Suffocated,
His brain seems to be running out of air.
Took up the profession he hated,
Trapped is he in society's lair.

Calypso

Once upon a time, in a not-so-far-away land,
A girl was born to a family not that grand.
Her wails and cries rented the air,
While her begetters looked at the thing without a care.

From then her story began,
No, not like Snow White with rabbits that ran,
Or Cinderella whose glittering shoes changed her life,
Nope, not any of them, all her life was filled with strife.

First, she was refused erudition,
"Okay," she said, "At least give me nutrition."
Persecuted and marred she was for her demands,
A beauty trapped in an island, a Calypso with shackled hands.

Calligraphy

Etched in our hearts,
Are the songs sung by our past.
A past that has grown up,
No longer drinking cola from plastic cups.
We sing this song everyday,
To its melody and rhythm we sway.
Hearts full,
Our eyes, a zillion memories rule.
Clasped hands and humming lips,
We give each other a good-bye kiss.
An irreversible promise to meet again soon,
Proud of our love, we look at the good-old moon.
My soul's complete,
With his perfect imperfections, nothing can compete.
Written in our hearts are three words,
Imprinted, capable of moving millions of Earths.

Burning Bridges

Sometimes,
distance brings us closer
than we were ever meant to be.
Like tendrils of a flower,
reaching out,
rekindling the fire that was once put out.

Blue

What's blue they ask,
I say, "Everything it shrouds, everything it masks."
From critters to huge beasts on land,
All of them, every single one seems sad.
"Mom, why is the sky blue?" she asked,
It's because of the choking air, she coughed and she rasped.
Is there any end to this?
Yes, first the feet of Mother Nature you must kiss,
She has given us mountains enough to fit oceans,
And oceans vast enough to give sailors a notion of
helplessness.
Then why do we whack at her, why do we chop,
"Pull her down! Tie her with a rope!!"
Haha, little do they realize,
They are bringing about their own demise.

Acidic

She hates her friends,
It is so damn hard to make amends.
Dad and mum despise her,
She is their daughter, a.k.a, a complete failure.
Boyfriend?
Sugar-coated poison daily he sends.
Siblings are amazing, right?
Blackmails and malevolence haunts her, every single night.
She hates herself,
Anger, envy, disgust; these are the "trophies" up her shelf.
Wants to end her,
Finally, she can call herself a murderer.

A Knight in Shining Armor

I thought
that you were
my knight in shining armor.
Turns out,
you had
put on
an armor
to shield yourself
from my demons.

You are no knight.

Alpha and Omega

The first time I saw you,
You never had a mask.
Oh, I loved those eyes so very blue,
Never knew they held everything but the truth.

The last time I saw you,
The mask was thrown away.
My love and heart you forsook,
Sucked the breath out of my lips, all the colour for yourself you took.

Anchor

Buried we are under an ocean of books,
Not having time to care about gossip or looks.
But to redeem us, God sent us saviours,
"Teachers" we call them, our ships they anchor.

Artifice

Lie upon lie she said,
And slowly he watched her, his eyes going red.
Darling, sin begets sin,
Don't do this to your kin,
Why this mask,
I can't quite understand,
It's me, my love, not any other man,
Slowly I hear my heart crack,
Yes, it is love that I lack.
Lie after lie she said,
And crying he went to bed.

Backspace

How I yearn
to send
all those
unsent,
random,
raw,
messages to you.

Blame Game

Roses are red,
Violets are blue.
If I was found dead,
I'd blame you.

3 AM

She missed him
on the
freezing,
cold,
blanket-less nights,
wishing for someone
to hold her close
and rock her
back to sleep.

Let Him Go

Listen to my pleas! Oh, will you?
This man I bind, his heart is true,
Let him go, he's done no crime,
In hope and faith, I sing this rhyme.

Remove my locks from his hands bloodless,
If shackles could talk, I would prove him innocent,
Somewhere in a tavern the trespasser hides,
Don't crucify this lad, in purity his soul lies.

Break me into pieces so he shall be free,
I see what no soldier can ever see,
A heart of gold encased in flesh and bones,
Let him go, he has done no wrong to the throne.

I weep for him as his blood stains me,
My voice cannot be heard; not one's ear it reach,
"Don't cry!" I say to the child that wails,
As my faith in faith his death curtails.

Paranoia

Don't you dare step out of line,
Don't you ever think about being anyone else's but mine.
Don't get out of the house at ANY cost,
Don't read, for heaven's sake, my dignity will be lost!
Don't be anything else but good,
Don't look through my papers (*what would you understand anyway?)*, just cook!
Do me a favour,
Be an impeccable wife, no other interest you shall foster.

Taped Up

Stop giving excuses,
Let me go if I'm a nuisance,
Stop making me yearn for a backup parent,
Please, don't leave me alone; for my sanity I fend.
Tie me up and hear me say,
"I was alone, and you were away,"
Throttle me until I moan,
"Why can't you see my heart's woebegone?"
Call me needy,
I *need* love; I've lost so much already.

But you've taped me up, so I can't speak.
Hear me out, for once. Please.

Too Busy

Why are you so entangled in life's vines,
That you have no time left for me?
My smile fades as you stare at your phone every single
time,
I'm bleeding, can't you see?

Unheeded voices,
I nevertheless implore, "Listen!"
No one to turn toward when crisis
strikes, I falter as you deafen.

www.ingramcontent.com/pod-product-compliance
Lightning Source LLC
LaVergne TN
LVHW090138160826
845673LV00017B/2513

* 9 7 8 9 3 8 9 5 4 0 0 2 4 *